In Heaven's Light

In Heaven's Light

Psalms and Spiritual Poetry

Denise M. Barbour

Pleasant Word
A Division of WINEPRESS PUBLISHING

© 2008 by Denise M. Barbour. All rights reserved.

Pleasant Word (a division of WinePress Publishing, PO Box 428, Enumclaw, WA 98022) functions only as book publisher. As such, the ultimate design, content, editorial accuracy, and views expressed or implied in this work are those of the author.

No part of this publication may be reproduced, stored in a retrieval system, or transmitted in any way by any means—electronic, mechanical, photocopy, recording, or otherwise—without the prior permission of the copyright holder, except as provided by USA copyright law.

Unless otherwise noted, all Scriptures are taken from the Holy Bible, New International Version, Copyright © 1973, 1978, 1984 by the International Bible Society. Used by permission of Zondervan Publishing House. The "NIV" and "New International Version" trademarks are registered in the United States Patent and Trademark Office by International Bible Society.

ISBN 13: 978-1-4141-0916-9
ISBN 10: 1-4141-0916-4
Library of Congress Catalog Card Number: 2006910529

Table of Contents

Foreword ix
Introduction xi

1. Words from the Vine 13
2. Meet Me in a Holy Place 15
3. Search Me 17
4. A Mother's Tribute to Her Children 19
5. If Something Were Left 21
6. Come into His Presence 23
7. Disillusioned Disciple 25
8. The Song of My Heart 27
9. Don't Give Up 29
10. Wrestle 30
11. Wrestling vs. Accepting 32
12. First Sight of Baby 35
13. Morning Praise 37
14. Birth, New Life, and a Fresh Start 39
15. Betrayed by the Body 41
16. Your Image 43

17. I Trust in You, Lord 44
18. A Stone to Throw 46
19. Thankfulness: A Choice 48
20. Purest Gold 50
21. Come to Me Early 51
22. If We Knew… 52
23. You're the One I Need 54
24. Struggle 55
25. My Face 56
26. A God Given Name 58
27. Come in Corporate Worship 59
28. Journey Toward New Life 60
29. New Life 62
30. Make a New Covenant 64
31. The Pulse of Life 66
32. Put on New Garments 68
33. Called by a New Name 70
34. I Make All Things New 72
35. Hard Living Transformation 74
36. Prayer for Birth 75
37. It Hurts 76
38. Overcome Impurity 78
39. Your Presence 80
40. He's Most Near 81
41. Meat 83
42. The Shepherd 84
43. You're Lying 86
44. Prayer Introspection 88
45. Treasure Offering 90
46. The Graduate 91
47. Gift in Trial 93
48. Breathe on Me 95
49. Morning Meeting 97

50. His Call 98
51. A Second Witness of Christ? 100
52. Life, a Never-Ending Poem 102
53. Too Many Trials 104
54. Touch the Thorn 106
55. Hush 109
56. I Seek to be Transformed 111
57. Your Walk, Our Walk, His Walk 112
58. You're More Than Dear 115
59. Closer Than a Friend 118
60. Even to the Least 120
61. Lord, I Love You 122
62. 23rd Psalm Makeover–Shepherd to Parent 123
63. Pray Like Angels 125
64. Stand 127
65. There was a Cross 129
66. There's a Fire 130
67. Prisons 132

Index by Topic 141
   Alphabetical Index 144
Order Form 147

Foreword

This collection of poetic thought and insight brings the soul in tune with God. It turns the ordinary to sacred, it transforms the mind to temple, and shifts the mundane to spiritual. It frees us from outward attachments that hinder the internal gaze of soul upon God and releases us to turn our will toward God.

Reading my dear friend Denise's psalms and spiritual poetry, alters the moment for me. I experience the Holy Spirit's presence in my soul and see God's wonder all around me as I read her inspired words. The struggles of life, the questions of eternity, the frustrations of time and place, all reflect Denise's faith journey, a journey that lives, breathes, and speaks of God's grace and presence. For me, her words are modern-day-David psalms and prayers. In them I can hear her laughter, feel her tears, and listen to her sing faithful words of hope as she shares her authentic expressions and reflections on being a wife, mother, friend, and disciple of Jesus Christ.

I pray that her words will inspire you as they have me to go deeper in my relationship with Jesus, who calls me and you to follow him. May this word treasure open your soul to talk with God, allowing you to meet Christ "in a Holy Place" where he calls and waits for you.

Linda L Bosch

INTRODUCTION

If you are like me, you may not even pause to read this introduction, hurrying on to find out what's inside. But if you've taken a moment, this is what I'd say to you.

If you took a look through my book shelves at home, you would not find books and volumes of poetry. I am not particularly drawn to read or write poetry for the sake of reading or writing poetry. However, if you peruse my prayer journals, poetic words appear on many pages. Actually, my poetic expressions were first seen in song. I have included the beloved words to my song, "Meet Me in a Holy Place." Plus, I've slightly altered a few of my songs to include their messages here. And I must ask your indulgence as I felt compelled to include the song, "Prisons," with its chorus. I purposely chose to include the chorus to repeatedly declare the power of its message. Though a song, though a poem, it is mostly "a message." It has too many verses to sing or recite, but not nearly enough to exhaust Christ's ability to liberate. And though this is a book of poems, they are mostly messages. Set to rhyme, spoken in rhythm, but above all, they are messages. Spirit-inspired messages.

I will also tell you I have chosen to capitalize any and every word that refers to God Almighty, Jesus Christ and the Holy Spirit, but to leave lower case any reference to the adversary. This is deliberate. Whether it is considered grammatically correct, I care not. It is eternally correct and I hope you will find your reverence to our Lord capitalized as you notice these structures throughout the book.

It is my prayer that as your life's journey meets the pages of this book, the Holy Spirit will breathe words of encouragement, hope, wisdom and instruction into your soul. Because that is what the Spirit accomplished in me when I first heard these words whispered into my heart.

Oftentimes pages of pondering and/or teaching followed or preceded the writing of particular poems. I've only included such additional thoughts with the poem "Wrestle." But I hope you will be open to allowing the Spirit to take you into personal discourse and/or journaling whenever a particular message strikes a resonating chord in your soul.

It is not in effort or from desire to be known as author, poet, or songwriter that I present to you this book. I would much rather be known as the Spirit's friend. And it is to that precious hope that I will continue to pursue the moments, in relationship, that birthed these writings.

May God richly bless your journey to know Him better as you read, ponder, and personally experience the poems and messages to come.

denise

Words from the Vine

Why's the word "poem" something I don't like?
Does it reek of frivolity, appearing too trite?

'Cause when I hear You, in words, oh, so clear
They often come poetically, precious, and dear.

And Your words, they never are trite or blah, blah.
They're powerful, life changing, filling with awe.

Yet, poem they are, and poet I am
When I sit at my journal, and put them to pen.

So, why so aversive do those titles seem?
Would lyricist or psalmist suit better my dream?

Whether lyricist, or psalmist, or poet, or more,
I'll write what I hear, whispered at my heart's door.

In Heaven's Light

So join in, my friend, ponder words set to rhyme.
They're poems. They're heart songs.
They're my fruit from the Vine.

I pray they will edify. I hope they will bless,
As you steal quiet moments, in solace and rest,

To feed your dear spirit, with words from the Vine
Some fruit God is sharing 'tween your heart and mine.

©2006 Denise M. Barbour

Meet Me in a Holy Place

Meet Me in a holy place.
>Meet Me in the busy race.
>>Find the time to seek My face.
>>>Meet Me in this place.

>>Meet Me in a holy place.
>Seek Me now, don't hesitate.
>Meet Me when all time and space,

Would call you far from Me.

Meet Me in a holy place.
>Seek to see Me face to face.
>>Deep within there is a place,
>>>I will wait for you.

In Heaven's Light

I'll meet You in a holy place.

    I'll meet You in the busy race.

        I'll find the time to seek Your face.

            I'll meet You in this place.

            I'll meet You in a holy place.

    I'll seek You now, I won't hesitate.

    I'll meet You when all time and space,

Would call me far from You.

I'll meet You in a holy place.

    I'll seek to see You face to face.

        Deep within there is a place,

            I will wait for You.

                © 1997 Denise M. Barbour

SEARCH ME

Search the *stable* in my soul
Find in there who's in control
May the *Babe* born years ago
Be found there in my soul.

Search the *temple* of my mind
Find the *Boy* who stayed behind
May His wisdom flow in me
And teach eternity.

Search the *desert* of my heart
Find in there the driest part
Let the *Man* who overcame
Within my desert reign.

Search my *raging storm* of will
Speak into it "Peace Be Still."
Let the *Voice* that calmed the sea
Bring godly harmony.

In Heaven's Light

Search me in *life's waning hour*
Roll the stone and show Your power
Send *Your Son* who conquered death
Eternal life to bless.

© 2000 Denise M. Barbour

A Mother's Tribute to Her Children
Shara, Misha, Collin, Caitlyn, Victoria, and Landon

You are a miracle! You are a gift!
You are a blessing from God!
You are amazing! A wonder of life!
You are a gift from above!

Your talents, your calling, the days you will live
They're all known to God, in His love
The incredible asset you are to His sheep
It leaves me in awe from above.

And just from the small glimpse that I've seen of you
I smile, and I tremble, and cry.
To think that the Lord with the world in His hands,
Would send you to one such as I.

To hold you, to mold you, encourage and love.
To watch as He works out His plan.
The honor, the joy, just to see in your eyes,
The trust that you put in my hand.

In Heaven's Light

For God to allow me a part in your life
And not from the back or the side
But sitting right smack in the center front row
Support for you, I cannot hide.

You're mine. Sure, I claim you! And yet I know bett'r
For how can I own what is God's?
A miracle acknowledged. A blessing received.
A gift given me against odds.

©2001 Denise M. Barbour

If Something Were Left

If something were left that I hadn't yet given
If something were left that I hid from Your face
If something lay hidden more precious to treasure
I gladly now put it in its rightful place.
At Your feet!
At Your feet, I lay my treasure.
At Your feet, I give it to you.
Please take it and hold it and keep it forever.
For none will I treasure more highly than You.

If something were left that I've yet to surrender
If something were left that I hoped I could hide
If something desired my heart's love forever
I gladly release it, to be at Your side.
At Your side!
Oh, to be there forever.
At Your side, I ever would be.
Please take me and hold me and keep me forever.
For none could I stand by more Holy than Thee.

IN HEAVEN'S LIGHT

If something were left that I hadn't yet noticed
If something were left that kept me from grace
If that something desired that I leave it unnoticed
I gladly will hunt it for my Savior's face.
For Your face!
Lord, the joy I can't measure.
Your face, shine on me, I pray.
I won't keep from You, my heart's love or treasure.
I won't choose another, through all of my days.

©1998 Denise M. Barbour

Come into His Presence

Come into His presence.
    Come into the hall.
        Come into His presence,
            That you might hear the call.
I will sing it to this people,
    With the voice I have to give.
        Come into His presence,
            That you might truly live.

Come into His presence.
    Come in at the gate.
        Come into His presence.
            I pray you won't be late,
For the Lord of Hosts is waiting,
    And yet not patiently.
        He is standing at the doorway
            Standing there for you and me.

In Heaven's Light

Come in with thanksgiving.
    Come to Him with joy.
        Come to be a blessing,
            All God's children, girl or boy.
For the Lord of Hosts is waiting,
    And yet not patiently.
        He needs us in His presence.
            He needs both you and me.

                        ©1998 Denise M. Barbour

Disillusioned Disciple

Who are you, man of Jerusalem?
Are you a man or the Great I Am?
Are you the one they say you are?
Are you man, or God? I have to know!

I saw you feed five thousand on a hill.
I heard you make the waves and wind be still.
How can it be that a man can do all this?
Are you man, or God? I have to know!

Your words astound.
They heal, they free, they bless.
Your words are fire. They burn upon my breast.
How can it be a man can speak like this?
Are you man, or God? I have to know!

You knew the night they would take you away.
You could have stopped it all along the way.
Why did you go? Why did you choose to leave?
Are you man, or God? I have to know!

In Heaven's Light

Now I stand before a cross on Calvary,
Half in shock and wonder at how all this could be.
Never have I felt a grief as great as this.
Are you man, or God? I have to know!
Are you man, or God? Please tell me so.

Lost in my sorrow, I hardly feel your hand.
Laid on my shoulder that I might understand.
When I turn around Your eyes again I see.
They're the eyes of God looking at me.
With the eyes of God, You look through me.

How can it be You're standing at my side?
So many questions, I cannot abide.
One thing is true, You're more than just a man.
You're the Great I Am, and now I see.
It's the Great I Am, right here with me.

Who is this man of Jerusalem?
Is he a man or the Great I Am?
You need to know. You need to ask Him too.
"Are You man? Are You God?"
You have to know!
And the One True God will tell you so.

©1998 Denise M. Barbour

The Song of My Heart

If I could sing a song to You,
How would that song begin?
How would I choose to tell to folks
The blessing You have been?

Would I count the many ways
My life's been filled with joy?
The laughter, friends, amazing things,
The honors won, the noise?

Or would I tell of harder times
When all was pain and blue?
Times when none could ease my hurt,
No one, that is, but You.

Maybe it would be the times
When I felt all alone.
The desert land, the long dry spells
When You became my home.

In Heaven's Light

A home of solace and of peace.
A home for healing dear.
A place to go to rest and reach
For more than is down here.

"Where is this place," they now may ask.
"A place of love divine?"
"Where is a place to be in joy
Or pain of heart and mind?"

This place you seek, this place I know,
Is in the heart of God.
This place is dearer to my soul
Than any I have trod.

And you, my friend, can enter too.
The entrance fee is free.
The Lord of Hosts awaits you now.
Come one, come all, come see!

©1998 Denise M. Barbour

DON'T GIVE UP

Don't give up! He sees your sorrow.
Don't give up! He knows your pain.
Don't give up!
The One who gave you life
can bring you life again.

So just give it all to Jesus.
Give Him sorrow. Give Him pain.
Give Him ALL the things that bind you.
Become NEW in Jesus' name.

©1998 Denise M. Barbour

WRESTLE

Sometimes…

My Word you must work for,
    So wrestle it through.
My message is hidden,
    But still there for you.

"Don't leave without blessing!"
    Is what Jacob said.
Is it blessing or knowledge,
    Or healing, you beg?

For our time together
    Is no better spent,
Than in honest wrestling,
    So intimate.

In Heaven's Light

I love you to praise Me,
    And share your requests.
I love when you're tired,
    And draw near to rest.

But only a dear friend
    Will wrestle and stay.
Struggle in agony
    And not go away.

Sometimes it appears that
    I have left your side.
But do you hear, "Wrestle!
    And in Me abide!"

For that's what I'm saying.
    Now be true with Me.
Bare heart, mind, soul, body.
    Receive your blessing!

©2006 Denise M. Barbour

Wrestling vs. Accepting

My mind just rested upon a dear, vibrant Christian disciple and acquaintance. She is going through some scary and tough health issues and has asked for prayer. As I was thinking of her strong faith and potential responses to what has befallen her, I pondered these thoughts.

Now, if God's promise is true, that "all" things work to the good of those who love and serve God, then this debilitating condition couldn't have His permission to rest on her unless He could use it for her good. So, one God-trusting, faithful response could be to accept whatever is going on, however painful, however lifestyle-altering or even life-threatening, as somehow "good" in God's realm and press on.

Or as in my poem, "Wrestle!" even with the truth of the words from Scripture, God honors and even invites us to wrestle with Him over situations, lessons, life, and health issues.

What could be gained by either response in the realm of "relationship" with God?

Good solid, quiet trust could actually depersonalize God out of one's journey, even as it sets Him in the place of sovereignty. But wrestling it through, pressing in for understanding, or blessing, or endowment, or sweet release, requires close interaction of mind, close contact of heart, and close physical proximity with God.

A choice to "accept and trust" may diminish anxiety and foster equilibrium of inner peace. But a choice to wrestle; *that* can gain experiential "relationship" above and beyond the hoped-for blessing! Relationship with the One True God. And oh, how the heart of God longs for relationship with us. Since the moment of creation, He has desired close, intimate relationship with the creation He made in His image, desiring friends above slaves, servants, puppets, or remote control robots. Maybe the very calamity, crisis, or trial we're in is an invitation more to the relationship gained in wrestling than to the relocation to the valley of suffering, death, or despair.

How is it trials and suffering can strengthen faith and prove a reason to rejoice when Christ is revealed, except that they make us more like Him from sharing more with Him? Not so much in that we've both endured struggles, but that we've experienced them "together." And in wrestling, we experience them "together" in multiple aspects like the facets of a brilliantly-cut diamond.

Wrestle in the realm of heart—grow closer to God's heart.
Wrestle in the realm of intellect—gain godly intelligence.
Wrestle in the realm of body and soul—gain God's perspective on the physical realm.
Wrestle in the realm of the spiritual unknown—gain prophetic insight.
Wrestle with the limitation of physical frame and health—gain healing in your wings.

Wrestle! The more aspects in which you encounter or meet God in wrestling, the more aspects of you that will be intimately made aware of God.

Wrestling requires interest, focus, intent, exertion of effort, and engagement.
You can't nonchalantly wrestle!
You can't wrestle on the back burner!
You can't wrestle while pursuing another interest or activity. Nor can you wrestle by accident.
Wrestle with God! Gain intimate relationship with God.
Wrestle!

First Sight of Baby

She wiggled. She danced.
    She waved with her might.
'Cause today was the day of
    Her mommy's first sight.

First sight of her body
    First sound of her heart
Her mommy would witness
    Her baby's bright start.

But bright's not the prominent
    Feeling for mom.
She's worried. She's scared.
    Alone and withdrawn.

True, mom's choices brought her.
    But mom didn't expect,
A baby to follow,
    At least not just yet.

In Heaven's Light

But, alas, she is here.
      And soon mom will decide,
Will this baby continue
      Her dance deep inside?

So today we are gathered
      In an ultrasound room,
To wonder of wonders
      Peer inside a womb.

And mother's emotions
      May whirl to and fro
But to front center stage
      Her baby now goes.

So dance, my young beauty
      And pray with your might.
Know we here at Birth Choice,
      Join you in your plight.

And momma, don't fret
      We're here for you too.
There's more than one choice
      That's open to you.

©2006 Denise M. Barbour

MORNING PRAISE

Lord, it's the newness of morning.
This place is so quiet. And yet, I'm awake in the stillness.
Is it You Who beckons me from sleep?
Is it the sweetness of Your promise of presence that draws me here?

You are my God and yet a friend;
    a friend closer than a brother,
      more dear than an earthly parent,
      more precious than the most anointed teacher.
You've harbored me in Your safe harbor
    and my life is Yours.
You give me more than riches
    and You supply my every need.
You are great!   You are marvelous!
    Your works are without end!
And yet, You esteem me,
    the small workmanship of Your hand,
    as worthy of Your presence.

In Heaven's Light

I am honored.   I am humbled.
    I am submitted to be Yours,
        Oh, Great One of the Universe.

In this moment of sweet stillness,
In this moment of fragrant solitude,
Please speak, Your servant is listening.

Enlighten my understanding to hear
            You, and only You, this day.

My mighty God, in the name of Jesus, I pray. Only You.

                              ©1998 Denise M. Barbour

Birth, New Life, and a Fresh Start

(This poem was written when I was seven and a half months pregnant and the night before my ordination and my daughter's baptism.)

With each push of a tiny foot across my womb…
>I am reminded of impending
>Birth, New Life, and a Fresh Start

As the clock ticks ever closer to tomorrow's ordination…
>I fully expect the dawning of
>Birth, New Life, and a Fresh Start

As I see the anticipation in Caitlyn's face for tomorrow's baptism…
>I witness the excitement of
>Birth, New Life, and a Fresh Start

As I contemplate serving my first communion in the Lord's house…
>I share with many, the joy of
>Birth, New Life, and a Fresh Start

In Heaven's Light

As I walk through life with my Lord…
>I am ever invited to experience
>Birth, New Life, and a Fresh Start

>©1999 Denise M. Barbour

Betrayed by the Body

Betrayed by the body, is just how I feel.
And the vision of such would make your head reel.

A body assessing a member to toss!
One piece of the whole that it wouldn't mind lost!

Can you imagine the sight of the thing?
A man or a woman determining

An arm, a leg, an eye, an ear
Or something internal no more to want near?

It's ghastly, barbaric, if seen in the flesh
A body dissecting itself, as if best.

And how is it best to chop up and divide
The Body of Christ,
Whom He's called as His bride?

In Heaven's Light

She's called not to sit and wait till He comes,
He needs us to work, until the day's done.

But if the body dismembers herself,
Stays busy all day, pointing fingers in stealth,

With not just a point, but a whack and a slice,
All beat up and wounded, who could she entice?

The Bridegroom shan't marvel
Or swoon at her sight,
More likely He'll break down
And cry for her plight.

To see His bride wounded and torn to the core,
Is painful enough, but to know that the foe

Who wielded the blows cutting her to the quick
Was not an enemy, but her own judgment stick.

And in all those pieces, that great disarray,
Is there even a chance she can work till that day?

For work to be fruitful, for beauty to shine,
The bride must in unity to Christ realign.

©2006 Denise M. Barbour

Your Image

Your image, Your image, fashioned with care.
Of all of the creatures, none can compare,
To the one You made true to Your image so fair.

Your image, Your image, how great, how divine.
No creature, no fowl, no herb from the vine,
Totes the image of God for Your purposeful design.

But we of Your image, we wander and play.
We waste precious moments of Your given day.
How can we not see, when we look in the mirror,
The reflection of greatness, so far, yet so near.

Endow us, O Lord, with eyes that will see,
'Tis You, all along we were made like to be.

©1996 Denise M. Barbour

I Trust in You, Lord

Though I do not know what tomorrow may bring
I trust in You, Lord, and my heart's free to sing.

Though I cannot see the road up ahead,
I trust in You, Lord, and all You have said.

Though I cannot choose the way for my young,
I trust in You, Lord, that Your work there's begun.

Though I cannot make life's pains go away,
I trust in You, Lord, to get through the day.

Though many a mile will pass under foot,
I trust in You, Lord, for the prize, it is worth.

Though times may get hard and skies can turn gray,
I trust in You, Lord, to show me the way.

In Heaven's Light

Though tired and weary I may find my head,
I trust in You, Lord, to intercede by my bed.

Though the day will come when this life I will leave,
I trust in You, Lord, my way home, You will lead.

©1999 Denise M. Barbour

A Stone to Throw

Lord, I'm holding my stone again in my hand.
I need You to write words to me in the sand.

I'm holding it tight, but it wants to take flight.
I sought out this rock, just to throw with my might.

I'm angry, hurt, mad, and I know who's at fault.
The vices that plague me will be hushed with this rock.

I know if I throw it right at the culprit,
The relief that I need will result when it hits.

It's blame that I want to hit squarely on them.
"It's their fault! Not mine! I demand this to end!"

But what? Are You writing to me, in the sand?
Your words, full of grace, make the rock leave my hand.

Not thrown with my might, but dropped at my side.
The stone now seems pointless, my motives I'd hide.

In Heaven's Light

But You've seen my heart, my motives You knew.
And You intervened, 'cause I asked You to.

Your message is clear if we take time to read
In the Book or in sand, there's still hope to be freed.

Freed not just of sins that we hurt others by,
But freed of our stones, used to hurt and divide.

Our stones are our judgments we so quickly pick up.
Our throw is the sentence, which leaves both of us crushed.

But Your way is higher than crush and destroy.
It feels, oh, so different. But I'll try to employ

Your new way of thinking of those who offend,
Miss the mark and fall short, them, I will defend.

And place them quite squarely in front of Your feet.
My stone will free no one. It's You we must meet.

Stone thrower and stoned, neither is sin-free.
We both need a Savior. Free them and free me!

©2006 Denise M. Barbour

THANKFULNESS: A CHOICE

Lord, thanks for dirty dishes.
They have a tale to tell.
While other folks are hungry,
We're eating very well.

And thank you for the dirty clothes
I found under the bed.
For all my children are well clothed
And none must go naked.

Thank you for those unmade beds.
A sight to see, they are.
But precious rest they bring each one,
Not like a mat of straw.

And thank you, Lord, for bathrooms,
With tiles that do not shine
And mirrors with streaky fingerprints,
Indoors, too close to whine.

In Heaven's Light

Lord, thank you for the slamming door,
And feet that run too fast.
For "outdoor" voices "in" my home,
Too soon are grown and past.

The chores that loom above my head,
Can drain me to the core,
Until I see your blessings there,
And thank you, Lord, once more.

©1999 Denise M. Barbour

PUREST GOLD

The purest gold faced the hottest fire.

My precious child, don't fear the fire.

The brightest diamond was cut and cut.

Oh dear, dear one, don't fear the cut.

The priceless pearl had a humble start.

My miracle child, don't despise your start.

If the Master holds you in His hands,

Then trust Him, child, and heed His commands.

©2006 Denise M. Barbour

Come to Me Early

Come to Me early. Come to Me late.
Come in your breath and your song.
Come in your tears and yearnings of late.
By this, you know you belong.

Now is the time. Now is the day.
Hesitation has passed.
Now is the moment. You must not delay.
Respond!
     Rejoice!
          And grasp!

Grasp *vision* I have for this land.

Grasp *hope* that's yours in the Lord.

Grasp *words* said by old and new.

Hang on, oh, my people. HANG ON!

©1999 Denise M. Barbour

IF WE KNEW...

If we knew how close we really were,
If we knew how close we could be,
If we knew how close we really were,
Would you lose you? Would I lose me?

Or would we reach a higher understanding?
Would we live upon a higher plane?
Would we move into a new dimension?
Of common hope and common pain?

If I knew how close to you I really was,
If I knew how close we could be,
If I knew how close to you I really was,
Would you lose you? Would I lose me?

Or would I find my truest presence?
Would I meet the deepest part of me?
As I see how we all fit together,
Can we be perfect harmony?

In Heaven's Light

If you knew how close to me you really were,
If you knew how close we could be,
If you knew how close to me you really were,
Would you lose you? Would I lose me?

Will you risk the fear of knowing someone?
Can I risk the fear of sharing me?
Will we step together into unity?
Unity that only God can be?

©2000 Denise M. Barbour

You're the One I Need

How can I find peace? How can I find joy?
How can I find You?
I fear my hope has been destroyed.

I need to feel Your touch. I need to know Your hope.
I need to have You here
'Cause I've no other way to cope.

You're the One I need
When I can see I've nothing left to give.

You're the One I need when I could run away.

You're the One I need when life is so unfair.

You're the One I need to show them that You care.

©2006 Denise M. Barbour

STRUGGLE

I struggle, you struggle, we struggle
    to see what the Lord has in mind.
And most often we never do see it,
    requiring the faith of the blind.

Is God orchestrating a mystery
    to be revealed in due time?
Or is satan just having a heyday
    messing with your life and mine?

In blind faith I choose to believe it,
    that God has a plan for our lives.
And satan may think that he's gaining,
    but in truth all he has are his lies.

So whether attacked or forgotten,
    confused or in prison detained,
Rejoice in the Only Begotten,
    for in Him you'll never be shamed.

©2006 Denise M. Barbour

My Face

You have come
>> a long way.
>>>> You will go
>>>>>> a long way still.

But My Face will sustain you.
To seek My Face is glory.
To know it
> without doubt,
>> in the flesh,
>>> is to live with Me
>>>> in eternity without end.
>> Seek the counsel of My Spirit.
>> Seek the countenance of My Face.
> In its sharpest detail you will see worlds without end.

In My Face are
>> My sorrows, My joys,
> My incomparable, all-consuming, compassionate love,
>> My chastisement and calling,
>>> the future and past.

In Heaven's Light

The Friend of the friendless is seen in My glance.
Read My Face.
Become accustomed to My facial language.
It will be a blessing to you
and
It shall be a gift of Me,
Ever present,
Ever communicating.

©1999 Denise M. Barbour

A God Given Name

Listen! Can you hear it?
Hear it whispered in the breeze.

Inhale! Can you smell it?
Such comfort drops you to your knees.

Reach out! Can you feel it?
Feel assurance deep within.

Open! Can you taste it?
Taste identity without sin.

Look now! Can you see it?
How a name completes the call.

Receive it! Oh dear loved one,
Receive your true name and stand tall.

©2006 Denise M. Barbour

Come in Corporate Worship

Welcome, My children,
I'm glad you have come.
And now in My Spirit,
You may become One.

Your worship is precious
Your praises are sweet.
Your prayer lifts to heaven,
And is placed at My feet.

In one heart and mind,
Now join and unite.
It's more than a focus.
Seek Me with your might.

As one soul by one
You find life new with Me,
The Zion you seek
Will become reality.

©2006 Denise M. Barbour

Journey Toward New Life

Lord, You have revealed to me how my heart holds habits that are counter to Your kingdom. So, please establish in me the "New" kingdom habit.

And oh, help! As I ask it, I realize to gain a new habit I must exercise the choice to *live* in the new habit when the old knocks at my door. And I dread feeling this way. This wounded way that precipitates my counter-kingdom behavior.

Yet, Lord, I yield myself to You.
I choose to step onto the Potter's wheel.

You are the Potter, I am the clay.
You see the vision for the way I should play.
I will not resist You,
I will not delay.
For You are the Potter, and I am the clay.

And next I see the Refiner's fire!
Oh, Refiner's fire! A hot place! A scary place!

In Heaven's Light

Revealing and surfacing the darkest, foreign, most anti-kingdom particles hidden deep within me.
The walk to the Refiner's fire is like a dirge.
The dread and the death rise up in me and threaten to thwart my steps.

But You beckon me toward holiness,
and I would not make You wait.

Refiner, You call me into Your fire.
Refiner, Your skilled hand has no fear of my mire.
Refiner, I answer You and continue Your way,
And step right on in, Your will to obey.

And now I am aware of the Physician's knife
at the time of surgery.

Why would one lie under the Physician's knife?
Unless one was certain it would yield a new life.

And though I am certain, I lie here in fear
As now draws the curtain on old ways I held dear.

Physician, Physician, Your tools hold the key
For hope of removing what's wrong inside me.
Wield swiftly Your knife with haste and with care.
Remove so completely what's wrong inside there.
If I'm to be given a new start at life
I know that I must go under the knife.
In fear and in trembling, I present myself
To the Hands of the Physician, Creator of health.

©2006 Denise M. Barbour

NEW LIFE

You call me to new life.
New life sounds so grand.
But new life and old life
Cannot live hand in hand.

For old ways must perish
If new are to thrive.
And the old I can't relish
If the new comes alive.

And as I draw near'r You, it grows painfully clearer
That it is not You that I see in my mirror.

Much death waits within me.
Much dross to be burned
Much which must be taken
Things given—things learned.

In Heaven's Light

Though I know I have loved You
And have You tried to serve,
The volume of ME found
Is nearly absurd.

And what will be left may not look much like me.
But is not that the point? To be clearly like Thee?

So to new life You've beckoned
And to new life, I come.
Let my life be reckoned
To the life of The ONE.

©2005 Denise M. Barbour

Make a New Covenant

Is there problem with the covenant,
    that God has made with us?
Is there need to find a new one,
    that causes all this fuss?

Or is the covenant,
    that He cut with you and me,
Sufficient for this time
    and all eternity?

For if there is no failing,
    in its power or deed,
The problem then appears to be,
    deep in you and me.

So make ANEW the covenant,
    within your heart and mind.
Make ANEW the promises,
    between His heart and thine.

In Heaven's Light

As though in presence at the start,
      with passion and intent,
Revisit that great moment
      when for you His Son was sent.

The sacrifice was given.
      His blood precisely spilled.
His name bestowed upon you.
      His promises He's filled.

So who's the lacking in this deal?
      Who's oft forgot the way?
'Tis us whose memory seems to wane.
      But faithful He will stay.

So, make ANEW the covenant.
      Stand in that spot again.
Grasp hands anew. Receive and give.
      Be ever changed, my friend.

                          ©2006 Denise M. Barbour

The Pulse of Life

The Pulse of Life is in the Vine
    The branches know His power.
The Vine in season calls each one
    To blossom into flower.

    Transform us, Lord, in heart and mind.
    Transform us in Your light.
    Enliven us to live in peace,
    In love, and joy, and might.

The Pulse of Life is in the Vine.
    Its branches to adorn.
The flower blossoms wane and fade.
    The fruit to be well formed.

    Transform us, Lord, in heart and mind.
    Transform us in Your light.
    Enliven us to live in peace,
    In love, and joy, and might.

In Heaven's Light

The Pulse of Life is in the Vine.
      The fruit to be made ripe.
By harvest or upon the ground
      Invigorating life.

      Transform us, Lord, in heart and mind.
      Transform us in Your light.
      Enliven us to live in peace,
      In love, and joy, and might.

As branch, be ye in fall or spring
      Or even winter's night,
The Pulse of Life within you
      Transforms you in His light.

      Transform, us Lord, in heart and mind.
      Transform us in Your light.
      Enliven us to live in peace,
      In love, and joy, and might.

So be in blossom! Be in fruit!
      And let your fruit be free!
It's for this cause He's in you
      And also within me.

©2006 Denise M. Barbour

Put on New Garments

We want to look our best.
    It's the day to meet the King.
We search our holy resumes
    To find enough good things.

    We pin them on our chests.
        We wear them on our heads.
    But, in the light of godliness,
        They couldn't wrap the dead.

The garments of our making
    Are only filthy rags.
Nothing to be proud of,
    Much more like garbage bags.

    But the King has seen our quandary,
        And offers us His best.
    The choicest, whitest linen,
        A covering for our breast.

In Heaven's Light

So will we trade our garments,
    Our filthy vain attempts
To look holy, to seem righteous,
    Instead to stand in His?

    Will we shed our self-made rags?
        Risk nakedness to see,
    The righteous, royal robes of whiteness
        Cover you and me?

'Cause for to make this trade divine,
    We'll have to strip and kneel.
We'll have to drop and leave behind,
    Things that used to feel so real.

    And in complete submission,
        With nothing much to boast,
    We'll kneel before the Holy One,
        And His Heavenly Host.

But in His grace and mercy,
    And to proclaim His Name,
Bolts of linen, pure and white,
    Roll out to clothe our frame.

    And in our garments, new and pure,
        He calls His saints, arise.
    "Arise in beauty, power, and strength!
        ARISE, My saints! ARISE!"

©2006 Denise M. Barbour

Called by a New Name
(Isaiah 62:1-5, Revelation 3:12)

Does the current name upon me
Incite pain, despair, distress?
Is the homeland of my household
Deserted and undressed?

For in truth it's aft' we've overcome
That sad and sorry state
Of being hated and despised
As our dear Lord's namesake

That then He looks upon us
And in voice profound and clear
He nullifies naysayers
With a name supremely dear.

A name declaring His delight
Erasing all the tears.
This name is whispered to each one
And's only for our ears.

In Heaven's Light

My new name is written on white stone
But known only to me.
And yours is written there as well
For only you to see.

This name not only heals us
But restores joy yet unknown.
Igniting who we are within
Even altering our home.

Renamed, we'll stand in glory,
In the homeland of our Lord.
Renamed, our home is Zion.
And from it we'll never roam.

So overcome, my brother!
My sister, ne'er give in!
New names await you in due time.
New names that come from Him.

©2006 Denise M. Barbour

I Make All Things New

Can you begin to catch the vision
Of what newness in you means?
Can you begin to feel the song sung
In your soul when newness sings?

And your heart in state of newness
Beats a new and brighter beat,
When the covenant of glory
Lights a new path for your feet.

So can you taste the fruits of newness?
Do you desire harvest fruit?
Can the pureness of new garments
Draw you closer to My truth?

Because it is in newness
Newness in you, through and through
That opens up your ears to hear
The new name I call you.

In Heaven's Light

And when all things are new
And the old has passed away
The memory of past things
Will seem miles and miles away.

For what matters in the newness
Is the fact that you're in Me
And that I am living in your midst
For all eternity.

But do not settle for this newness
To fall only on your wing
Spread the hope of fiery newness
Upon every living thing.

So Go, My children, swiftly!
Go in mercy, don't delay!
Let the newness that you've tasted
Spread to others. Start today!

©2006 Denise M. Barbour

Hard Living Transformation

I am lost. I am lonely. I'm mad at the world.
And I know that I hate it this way.
And you, all so fancy in diamonds and pearls,
You couldn't care less what I say.

Drive on by. Leave me lie in my pain.

I have fallen. Not really, 'cause I've never stood.
And you look at me though I've the plague.
How could I need anything that you have?
Though the house and the paycheck I'd take.

Touch me not. Leave me lie in my hate.

But you! You are different! What is this you say?
There's Someone who's not like the rest?
Your eyes do not shift, nor your hands pull away.
There's something I have to confess.

Something deep   in my heart that can't rest.
Something deep   in my heart cannot rest.

©1999 Denise M. Barbour

Prayer for Birth

O Great One of this earth,
Dare I still to ask for birth?

Yet it's birth again I seek.
Make me humble. Make me meek.

Make me all that Christ demands.
Birth my heart, my soul, my hands.

Take my life and make it new.
Make it more a part of You.

For upon this earth I'd stand
As a witness of the hand,

Of the Man who came and died
Who for sins was crucified

And Who rose on the third day
That His life might show the way.

©1999 Denise M. Barbour

It Hurts

"It hurts!" I told Jesus.
And I fell down to cry.
My heart was so broken,
My spirit so dry.

"I know," came His kind voice.
And He lifted my chin.
"I've been there my child.
And if you let Me in…

I'll take all those pieces,
Those broken, torn, shreds,
And weave them into something
Quite better," He said.

"I know it seems hard to
Imagine it true,
That something so bad,
Could bring good now to you.

In Heaven's Light

But that's what I'm saying,
And if you'll trust Me,
You'll see what forgiveness
And confession can bring.

The heart that's been broken
Heals deeper, it's true.
And the dryer the spirit,
The more precious the dew.

Add in some forgiveness,
Well, not some, but a lot,
'Cause that's how you'll get free
From this most painful spot.

I know you're not able.
Alone it's too hard.
So lean on Me, dear one.
Let go and trust God!"

©2006 Denise M. Barbour

OVERCOME IMPURITY
(REVELATION 21:1-7)

Overcome impurity
That you can be made new.
Overcome adversity.
He'll give His power to you.

Overcome temptation to
Feel fear or weak in faith.
Overcome that which would seek
All glory for its sake.

The vile, the murd'rers and immoral
And those who cling to sin
Who worship idols, call on ghosts,
And lie cannot come in.

But you who overcome the same,
Your home, your new abode,
Will be the very home of God.
You'll worship at His throne.

In Heaven's Light

'Cause after all the dead are judged
And hell has had its fill,
The righteous kingdom will come down,
And live with us, God will.

Its splendor will be dazzling.
Its glory without end.
As bride adorned in beaut'ful dress
The new Jerusalem.

All tears He'll dry within her.
And death will be no more.
Mourning and pain are passed away.
Thus ends the old order.

The Beginning and the End
Will say "Thirsty, come drink!"
And offer living water
From His never ending spring.

This royal declaration
That all things are made brand new!
Makes "new" all of creation
Including me and you.

©2006 Denise M. Barbour

Your Presence

Lord, I need to talk with You.
    Lord, You know I really do.
Not to share my list of needs
    Nor to fill Your ears with pleas.
But to listen and to share
    A wealth of friendship and Your care.

To hear You call me out by name
    To hear You chastise, calm, and tame
My fears, my worries, my straying ways
    To have Your presence through my days
What more is there to want or need?
    If not for that, what value greed?

Greedy, greedy to have more
    Greedy, greed-fill'd to the core
More of Your voice. More of Your peace.
    More of Your presence, please release.
So fill my heart with greed, oh, Lord
    For more of You till overflowed.

©2006 Denise M. Barbour

HE'S MOST NEAR

He's most near to the hurting
He's most near to the lost.
He's most near when the price exceeds the cost.

When a mother's heart is hurting,
When a father's heart falls numb,
When a waiting family's hope turns into fear,
When the One Whom you believe in
Turns His head to shed a tear,
It's the time when Jesus' Spirit is most near.

When the day begins in sorrow,
When the night drags on and on,
When the best thoughts you can think
Still leave despair,
When the truths that you have trusted
Are attacked beyond repair,
It's the time when Christ will show
How much He cares.

In Heaven's Light

When you find that you've been cheated,
When you feel that no one cares,
When it seems there's no way justice will prevail,
When the rules that you have followed,
Are discarded as junk mail,
It's the time when Christ will show He cannot fail.

He's most near to the hurting.
He's most near to the lost.
He's most near when the price exceeds the cost.

©2002 Denise M. Barbour

MEAT

Listen, my daughter, for listening is sweet.
And I will enliven your bones with sweet meat.

Milk has its place and blesses the young.
But My soldiers need meat and of them you are one.

Don't choke or dismay at the new taste or test.
For 'tis meat that you'll need before you'll find My rest.

What's meat, you may ask? How's it differ in taste?
How do I take it, and make sure not to waste?

Meat is the tough stuff, you may have to swallow.
Not easy commands and requirements to follow.

The stricter revealments and tighter patrol
Are because My army must stand and be whole.

So do not shy from harsh words, high demands
For they are required to transform the land.

©2006 Denise M. Barbour

THE SHEPHERD

Make His life your own. Give Him all your heart.
Know His voice alone. From it, don't depart.
'Cause when it boils down to the yeas and the nays,
It's His sheep who will enter, the others must stay.

"My sheep know My voice. They heed My command.
Past crevice and cranny, they move through the land.
I show them the way. Each sure-footed step.
I've guided their progress, so none would be left.

No tears shall they shed on the other side,
Though many a night they've laid here and cried.
They've grieved and they've mourned,
And lamented the loss,
Of those who chose darkness, instead of the cross.

In Heaven's Light

Their sorrow is Mine. But My joy is theirs too.
When all are called home, they'll find joy anew.
Don't worry and fret that that time isn't now.
But speed like the wind. Don't stumble on how.

Go make the last call. So My voice can be heard,
And more of My people can turn to My Word."

©1998 Denise M. Barbour

YOU'RE LYING

You say it doesn't matter that they never call.
You say you just don't care
They never meet you at the mall.
You say if it were different, you wouldn't notice it at all.

But all the time, you know you're lying.
You're lying.
Yes, all the time, you know
You're lying.

You say when they don't care to share a holiday
That they just are busy or don't feel good today.
You say when memories don't happen,
It's just better off that way.

But all the time, you know you're lying.
You're lying.
Yes, all the time, you know
You're lying.

In Heaven's Light

When your heart would break because
Your little ones miss love.
When hurt turns into hate and desires to berate,
So despair won't cause regret, do not act on it just yet.

'Cause in those angry words, you'd be lying.
You'd be lying.
Yes, all the time you know,
You would be lying.

So what's to do instead?
How to function in such dread?
Dread of your heart hurting more.
Dread of walking out the door.

How to bring in peace?
How to walk in sweet release?
How to speak the words of love without lying?
No more lying. No more lying.
Let me speak the words of love
Without lying.

Lord, help me speak Your words of love
Without lying.

©2006 Denise M. Barbour

Prayer Introspection

Is it peace I ask, or prosperity?
Is it all the things You can do for me?

Is it money, health, or a home restored?
Is it friends of wealth, who will me adore?

I sure have treated You as though,
You were there to serve me so.

But I must reach a higher plane,
One beyond my wants to gain.

Lord, I seek to know You there,
Not just a beggar for Your care.

Not to hoard Your blessings free,
But to stand as "friend" to Thee.

Not a friend who begs Your best,
For just myself and not the rest.

In Heaven's Light

But a friend who feels Your heart
And to others Your love imparts.

So purify my prayer to You,
And make our friendship ever new.

As much for Your sake as for mine,
Make my prayer life much more like Thine.

©2006 Denise M. Barbour

Treasure Offering

Take my heart. I say, I say. *(But of my money let ME play.)*

Take my life. I give it free. *(But of my cash, leave that to ME.)*

Take my time. It's "free" I say. *(But I can't help on a work day.)*

My talents and my gifts I bring.
I want the best to give my King.

My time. My talent. Life and heart.
What more could I give to show my part?

My treasure? Where I hold on tight?
My treasure? Where I most delight?

Oh me! Oh my! Could it be true?
Treasure's what I should offer you?

Gold and silver? Penny and dime?
Jefferson? Franklin? Or other kind?

Painful as this task may seem
I can and will, give for my King!

©2006 Denise M. Barbour

THE GRADUATE
(SHARA)

My baby's a graduate,
        About to take flight.
She's learned and she's studied,
        And gained with her might.

Not all of her lessons
        Were simple to learn.
Some came quite easy,
        Though others still burn.

But today as I see her
        All ready to fly,
I think of my baby
        And can't help but cry.

Not 'cause I've lost her,
        'Cause all this is gain.
And I'm proud as I see her
        Emerge through the rain.

In Heaven's Light

So many investments,
        My wisdom, my love
Are ready to take off
        With sights on above.

So fly my love sparrow
        Stretch wings, catch the wind.
Move on toward your calling.
        Watch closely for Him.

For God does not tarry
        A long way from you.
Much nearer than heaven,
        Directing you to

That calling, that purpose,
        That joy and delight,
That a soul in His service
        Experiences in flight.

When the wind that's beneath them
        Is blown from His throne,
There's no fear of crashing,
        You're never alone.

©2006 Denise M. Barbour

GIFT IN TRIAL

For a gift to be delightful
For a joy to be enjoyed
To feel gain in something given
Oft' a loss must be employed.

What's a friend
When you have plenty?
What is hope without despair?
What is peace if never trial?
What gain is a buck to a millionaire?

What is rest if you're not tired?
What's approval if all is well?
How precious trust if never stung?
Or being picked up if you never fell?

So we ought not cry in trial
For it works to make so sweet
The gift that's sure to follow
Those who worship at His feet.

In Heaven's Light

So whether storm or loss or tear
That beckons at your door,
Remember Christ is always near.
And it all will bless you more.

©2006 Denise M. Barbour

Breathe on Me

Breath above the wind.
      Wind above the sky.
           Where the Spirit blows is
                Deep in you and I.

Breathe on me Your breath divine,
    that I might know Your will.
Breathe on me Your breath divine,
    that I might love you still.

That's where the Spirit longs to blow,
    deep within our will
Changing our perspective
    for His love to be instilled.

Breathe on me Your breath divine,
    that I might want Your ways.
Breathe on me Your breath divine,
    that I might never stray.

In Heaven's Light

That's where the Spirit longs to blow,
        till desire is true,
Helping us to want no less,
        than all He's said He'll do.

Breathe on me Your breath divine,
        that I might see Your light.
Breathe on me Your breath divine,
        that I might want what's right.

That's where the Spirit longs to blow,
        even in our glance,
Changing eyes to see the Truth,
        in every circumstance.

        Breath above the wind.
        Wind above the sky.
        Where the Spirit blows is
        Deep in you and I.

        ©1998 Denise M. Barbour

Morning Meeting

Lord, have You called me?
Is it You who's stopped my sleep?
Is there something You would say,
Or is there an appointment we should keep?

For if Your voice is ready
Then my ears are ready more.
And if You have drawn near me,
Then I'll open wide the door.

Because there is no sweeter presence
In the whole wide world, I could
Spend a little time with.
None could ever be so good.

©2006 Denise M. Barbour

HIS CALL

He calls us to strengthen, encourage, obey.
A call to bring healing and peace in this day.
Know ye His voice. Yield to His command.
For that is sufficient to bring back His land.

His people are willing, if we show the way.
His Zion we're building. We can't stop to play.
The Spirit's sufficient to guide, to direct,
To teach, to enlighten, to chide the elect.

If we know that Spirit, we'll yield to His call.
All things shall be handled, both big and both small.
For His plan is perfect. His power complete.
In Him is no doubting, nor chance for defeat.

But if we're to stand in the stead of this One,
We can not be fearful. We cannot be glum.
We must walk with boldness, with joy and in power.
The words that we speak must bring love in this hour.

In Heaven's Light

No less will pierce through. No less can bring change,
To the coldest hard hearts, the blind, the deranged.
So reach for your armor. Sure it's a need!
But first, know your Savior, in heart, word, and deed.

©1998 Denise M. Barbour

A Second Witness of Christ?

Was there e'er a man named Alma?
Did Nephi ever walk the earth?
Were there servants in Amer'ca
Who declared the Savior's birth?

There is so much contention.
Judgments flair so hot and high,
Leaving to-the-bone division,
Among those who testify.

If there's only One Name given,
And that Name is Christ alone,
Is it logical to fight and
Feud o'er how Truth's seed is sown?

In Heaven's Light

If the Voice, the Word or whisper
Bid a human soul believe,
In the Holy One of Israel,
Then the message is Spirit-breathed.

So declare that Name in history.
Shout it loud in Bible print.
Dare not hush it in the current
From where'er the message's sent.

More important than the source,
More delightsome through and through.
Is the fact that Christ is held high,
To redeem both me and you.

We should banish words of judgment
And the fighting ought to end
As united in the Savior
We choose FIRST to follow Him.

And when believers join in heaven,
We shall meet them with the rest.
But no tears if they're just legend
'Cause it's Christ Who we confess.

©2006 Denise M. Barbour

Life, a Never-Ending Poem

There is sadness when a story is cut short.
But there is
CELEBRATION
in lives that do not end.

Life can neither end nor cease to be
when CHRIST is in the heart.

Our Christian lives are like never-ending poems.
    Poems which are "Master"fully being
created day upon day, into eternity.
    Not a short nursery rhyme, whose purpose is
only to be memorized and
    Recited on a small auditorium stage and
then the curtain closed,
    But a grandiose poem that is continuously
being created

    Performed in living, breathing, dancing
motion
        Upon the stage of the universe
      Whose curtain remains open for eternity.

In Heaven's Light

Each poem, while truly a sight to behold
in the flesh,
will whirl into
    an incredible,
        magnificent
            splendor
on the heavenly side of life's gate.

We must remember, it is **NOT** the Master Orator,
Nor the poem itself
That pauses to mourn for death.
For the life and the poem continue on
Without a missed beat.

Because, life is eternal through Christ.

And each poem,
    No matter how many earthly verses,
        Lasts an eternity.

And it's quite possible the *brightest* stanzas are
Expressed in *pure heavenly light*.

©1998 Denise M. Barbour

Too Many Trials

I just want to cry
        And for plenty of reasons.
How can it be
        That my faith is so fleeting?

The facts that surround me
        Bring tears to my eyes.
And so I feel numbness
        Around and inside.

I keep plodding on
        But my vigor has vanished.
I press on towards hope
        But my spirit is famished.

If I am to make it
        At Your feet I must fall.
I'd say it's to worship
        But I only can bawl.

In Heaven's Light

Then bawl's what I'll do
        And continue till done
For I know I'll feel bett'r
        At the feet of the One.

©2006 Denise M. Barbour

TOUCH THE THORN

A Poem for the healing of memories

When I walk the path of memory
There are flowers and there are thorns.
The flowers are so dear to me,
And yet there still are thorns.
Each flower has a special hue,
A color all its own.
Each blossom shares a memory
Of a seed that God had sown.

I love to gaze upon each flower.
The thrill I cannot hide.
As I joyfully recall the hour
Its petals opened wide.
Then my Savior pulled me close to Him.
His hand He held closed tight.
The smile that was upon His face
A strange, yet precious sight.

In Heaven's Light

And when He opened wide His hand
The thorn of yesterday
Its dreadful point was in His palm.
And I began to pray.
He held it, oh, so tenderly.
The thorn it dug so deep.
Not a painful frown.
But a searing smile.
And I began to weep.

He placed the thorn upon my path.
My path of memory.
Its dreadful point still dripped of blood.
My Savior's blood for me.
The thorn is now established there.
Its place and part to play.
Its sight brings pain. Its presence hard.
Reminder of the day.

But then I heard my Savior's voice.
I'm sure I heard Him say,
A shocking thing, a dreaded thing.
So I began to pray.
Then it came to me a second time.
His voice was bright and clear.
I knew I had to do His will.
And yet, I shed a tear.

In Heaven's Light

He pointed to a flower there
And also to the thorn.
I lovingly caressed the flower.
"And now," He said, "the thorn."
I couldn't bear the thought of it,
To touch that dreaded thing.
Its awful point. Its ugly pain.
To feel it once again.

"Now, touch the thorn."

So I reached my hand out to the thorn,
My Savior's hand on mine.
I felt the point. It still was sharp.
Till His blood mixed with mine.
When I looked down, my hand was healed.
The thorn, it had changed too.
Upon the ugly, painful thing
A bud began to bloom.

My garden path looks different now.
The thorns have gone away.
Because my Savior walks with me
Each and every day.
With His hand in mine, we search the path
For thorns still hidden there.
And when one shows its painful head,
His voice still says with care,

"Now, touch the thorn."

©1998 Denise M. Barbour

HUSH

(Psalm 46:7-11 "Be Still and Know That I Am God")

I should hush and so should you.
But do you know that scripture true

Is telling countries far and wide,
Large and small, on every side

To hush their clamor and their boast
To hush before the Lord of Hosts?

Hush and hear Him say, "Be still!"
Exalt Him ONLY, on the hill.

Hand over all your tools of war.
These works of evil are no more.

It's peace divine that will be heard,
When God Almighty says these words.

In Heaven's Light

Be still, and know that I am God.
I will be exalted, among the nations.
I will be exalted in the earth.
        Psalm 46:10

©2006 Denise M. Barbour

I Seek to be Transformed

Lord, I seek to be transformed!
What? You say it has begun?
Yea, I know that this is true.
For I do see more of You.
When I glance into the mirror,
When my heart would fail in fear,

Right there in my eyes I see,
Newness, deep inside of me.
A precious calm and piercing stare,
Of Holiness alive in there.
From my deepest depth of soul,
Lord, I feel Your thunder roll.

It stills and calms my darkest fears,
Yet truly humbles me to tears.
To know that You, Greatest of All,
Would pause to heed my heartfelt call,
And that You'd enter in my frame,
To bring more glory to Your Name.

©1999 Denise M. Barbour

Your Walk, Our Walk, His Walk
(Isaiah 61: 9)

Your life you live. Your life you give.
You give not of your own.
For all is Mine and Mine I share,
Through vessels I have honed.

Yes, you are Mine, and Mine is thine.
And on your walk you'll see,
As your heart grows into My heart
Your life shall tell of Me.

Walk steadfastly. Walk circumspectly.
Walk into the great unknown.
Your life will be, your life shall be
A flower from the throne.

Your walk need not be fearful
Nor need be clamoring great,
But be the quiet, gentle, power
Of One with perfect gait.

In Heaven's Light

My stride is yours. My walk your own.
My Spirit gives you peace.
Your footsteps bring a special sound
Announcing Princely feats.

Your walk today, your walk tomorrow,
Your walk a week from now,
Will all bring glory to the King,
That all might pause to bow.

A bow to honor not your form,
Not your feats, nor presence.
A bow to honor One alone.
The King of kings and peasants.

The One Almighty walks this earth
In form, by form, by form.
And you who've known the second birth
With power He will adorn.

You'll fall in line in unity,
To follow His command.
You'll walk alone. You'll walk as One.
You'll walk throughout this land.

All may not notice at first glance
Your strength or might or power.
But what they witness as you pass,
Will call them to this hour.

In Heaven's Light

"Please come along! The hour is here!
The time is short! Come now!"
This is the call you must cry forth.
"Repent! You have been found.

You are the one. And you alone,
Can choose to come or stay.
You hear His call! Now choose His way!
Join with the Lamb today!"

©1998 Denise M. Barbour

You're More Than Dear

Lord, I seek Your presence dear.
I long for You to hold me near.

    I want to live Your awesome life.
    I want Your knowledge and Your sight.

        I want to feel what's in Your heart,
        When others' actions hurt or smart.

            I want to see them through Your eyes.
            I want to cut through all the lies.

        The lies that satan seems to spread.
        The ones that fill us all with dread.

    They say we never will add up.
    We'll never love or care enough

To make this world a better place,
Imposs'ble for the human race!

In Heaven's Light

As always, there's a spot of truth.
For without You, what is the use?

    The pow'r is not in us alone
    Because it comes straight from Your throne.

    You give to us who do believe,
    A love beyond what we conceive.

    A love exceeding time and space.
    A love that saved the human race.

A love that entered as a Babe.
Then walked the human path You laid.

He taught. He healed. He spread Your Word.
He held the sins of all the world.

    He held them on a cross of pain.
    He did it so that life I'd gain.

    And when the angels brought Him home,
    It was in vict'ry, to a throne.

    A throne of glory and delight.
    A throne of never ending light.

    'Tis to this One, I bow my knee.
    For it is He who has saved me.

He conquered death. He conquered sin.
He conquered all. Then let me in.

In Heaven's Light

And if I give all that I am,
I can't begin to thank the Lamb.

    But still I shall try day and night,
    To do the things I know are right.

        But most I'll hold His Spirit near,
        Because to me, You're more than dear.

©1998 Denise M. Barbour

CLOSER THAN A FRIEND

When a friend is far away,
I need to hear You say
That Your love will see me through.
I can depend on You.

When I stand on foreign ground
and people wear a frown,
I need to know the place I stand
was made by Your mighty hand.

When the vision that I see
can be seen by only me,
I need Your reassuring hand,
that it's all within Your plan.

When I stand alone to fight,
I'll stand with all my might.
But when I feel my courage fail,
I need to know Your love prevails.

In Heaven's Light

For the love of God is closer than a friend.
And the land, the sea, the light, the sky, the wind,
All bear witness that You're near,
Witness that You're here,
Witness that the Spirit flows within.

©1998 Denise M. Barbour

Even to the Least

The very God of the universe,
Came to walk the earth as Man
He entered in as a Baby
In the town of Bethlehem.

Even though wise men and kings
Bowed before His bed,
The shepherds and the lowly ones
Bent to kiss His head.

On a hillside many folk
Came to hear the Gospel Man.
They gathered close, they pushed and shoved
In hopes to touch His hand.

The children, they could never hope
To see in such a crowd.
The men said, "No!" But Christ said, "Yes!
Bring them here!" He said it out loud.

In Heaven's Light

Even to the least of these,
The Father told the Son,
Even to the least of these,
That's how Our work is done.

He told them that His mission here,
Would soon come to an end.
That He would suffer and would die,
And that He'd rise again.

He told them that their hands and lives,
Would do the things He did.
Because He'd leave His Spirit here,
And in us, He would live.

Even through the least of these,
The Father told the Son.
Even through the least of these,
That's how Our work is done.

The saints stood 'round before the King,
On the day of judgment great.
They praised and worshipped Him aloud,
Upon His words they did wait.

He started to commend them for
The kindness showed to Him.
When they could not recall these things,
He said this unto them.

What you've done to the least of these,
You've done unto Me.
Even unto the least of these,
You've also done to Me.

©1998 Denise M. Barbour

LORD, I LOVE YOU

Lord, Lord, I love You, Lord.
You are my joy and my strength.

The sky is Your footstool.
The land is Your cloak.
The water Your joy overflowed.
The height of the mountain, Your majesty.
Your universe ever unfolds.

Your plan for salvation,
More precious than jewels.
Much better to wear than fine silk.
Diamonds and gold could never compare,
To the joy that You bring upon me.

Lord, Lord, I love You, Lord.
My joy and my strength are Yours.

©1998 Denise M. Barbour

23rd Psalm Makeover–Shepherd to Parent

The Lord is my Parent. I awake in His house.
He provides me with shelter and warmth.
My security, comfort, and needs are all met.
He's my Parent of great worth.

When my struggles surmount my ability to cope,
I crawl up into His lap.
And there I am held in His undying love
Until His hope fills my gap.

The talks and the walks through gardens and halls
Will ever endear Him to me.
For my Father alone knows the depth of my needs
And His child I will always be.

But even as children can fuss and can feud
Over trivial items and greed,
I stand oftentimes with my head hanging down
Expecting disgust for my deed.

In Heaven's Light

But each time I come to confess where I've been
He grabs me up into His arms
And there once again the desires of my heart
Are renewed in the joy of His charm.

His family name, its honor and note
Are on me because of His love.
With each passing year
I'll mature in His ways
Until the resemblance is clear.

If I look like My Father and speak as He speaks
If I see things the way that He does
If I walk in His footsteps at home and abroad
All will know I abide in His love.

He has protected me both day and night
Amongst those who would bring me harm
Calming my fears, sharing His light,
I will constantly feel His strong arms.

Through teaching and patience, He's shared who He is.
As Provider, He fills me with love.
As Comforter, He leads me into all peace.
He's the ONE Guide to heaven above.

©2006 Denise M. Barbour

Pray Like Angels

Many a message's been shared
Telling us the way,
What we're s'posed to do,
What we're s'posed to say.
But there is a question,
That's dear to God's own heart,
"Do you hear My voice?
Isn't it time you start?"

The streets of gold have caught the hope
Of many young and old.
But to journey there, my friend,
Is not just for the bold.
It takes an ear accustomed to
The Voice that speaks within.
"Come my child, the time is now.
Come, I call you in."

In Heaven's Light

So pray like angels.
Preach like Paul.
Heal like Peter did.
Bring them to the water.
Raise them from the dead.
The kingdom will bear witness
That what you've done is true.
But there is no greater joy
Than to hear Me speak to you.

©2004 Denise M. Barbour

STAND

Stand. Stand!
Stand where you've been planted.
Stand. Stand!
Stand where I've planted you.

There are times when you may wonder
    Just what I have in mind.
There are times when you may hardly see the way.
But the light that made the world begin
    Is by your side today
And I'll strengthen you and help you see the way.

There are reasons that you can't see
    For things that come your way.
There are times and seasons to each coming day.
But the world is Mine. And you will see,
    With each passing day,
That the plan is perfect when you just obey.

In Heaven's Light

I align My army, one by one,
> Just as I see the need.

You are one I need, right here, right now, indeed.
It's your work, your purpose, your desire
> To walk the walk I lead.

And I'll lift your head to stand your ground for Me.

So, Stand. Stand!
Stand where you've been planted.
Stand. Stand!
Stand where I've planted you.

©1997 Denise M. Barbour

There was a Cross

There was a cross that stood on a hill.
There was a time when all time stood still.
Bury that cross, deep in your heart.
Because of that cross, you get a new start.

There was a Man, who walked down the road.
Upon His back, He carried a load.
The load that He carried, included the cross,
The cross that would lighten the road for the lost.

You couldn't help Him, and neither could I.
Ten thousand angels stood silently by.
He had to carry the cross all alone.
So He could show us the way to get home.

Now is the time. Now is the day.
Do not postpone it, and go on your way.
What is the burden He bids you lay down?
Lay it down now in exchange for a crown.

©2000 Denise M. Barbour

There's a Fire

        There's a fire on the mountain.
      A lone shepherd sees.
    With fear in his heart,
He knows that's where to be.
When he reaches the fire,
    The Lord calls his name.
      And from that moment on,
        He is never the same.

There's a group of disciples
    In a closed room,
      Waiting for something
        They hope will come soon.
      They did not expect
    A fire and a wind
But it came just the same,
Now they stand for Him.

In Heaven's Light

There's a fire in this land.
A fire in this church.
Some understand.
Others still search.
There's a fire in our hearts,
Calling our names.
Let us stand in the fire.
We will never be the same.

From His fire on a mountain,
To His fire in a room.
Now He spreads through the land,
His church to consume.
Feel the blaze in your heart.
Hear Him call you by name.
Come and stand in His fire.
You will never be the same.

©1998 Denise M. Barbour

PRISONS

There's a prison on Susan,
And a prison on Paul
    It came from a needle
      She bought near the mall.
It promised her peace.
It promised her joy.
    But neither it's brought her.
    Now that she's sold her boy.

The prisons that hold us
Are broken by Christ.
The walls are torn down
By the power of His life.
No prison can keep us
When we ask Him in.
He's ready to free us.
The question is when.

In Heaven's Light

He's alone on a bar stool.
He's there every night.
    He looks fine by day.
    But he can't win the fight.
First she found another.
Then she took the kids.
    Now he drowns away,
    Any life left in him.

He sits on the sidelines,
His eyes full of tears.
    The put downs, the snide looks,
    The tauntings, the jeers.
The tears turned to mean looks,
The mean looks to fists.
    Now gangs, blood, and murder
    Are all on his list.

She dances for money.
She's the star of the show.
    She shows all her beauty
    Where the gentlemen go.
The glitz and the glamour
The suitors who pass.
    But one thing is missing,
    A love that will last.

But the prisons that hold us,
Are broken by Christ.
The walls are torn down
By the power of His life.
No prison can keep us
When we ask Him in.
He's ready to free us.
The question is when.

In Heaven's Light

She has a secret.
A secret she hides.
    She won't tell her mother,
    In whom she confides.
'Cause Daddy has told her,
That if she did tell,
    The good Lord of heaven,
    Would send her to hell.

It grips her by day.
And it grips her by night.
    When no one is watching
    She still feels the fright.
Her heart starts to pound.
Her hands start to shake.
    Soon nothing will calm
    The whimpers she makes.

They won't go to church.
No, not anymore.
    The hypocrites go there!
    What good is it for?
Offended, rejected,
And broken by strife.
    Though trials can strengthen,
    They're imprisoned for life.

But the prisons that hold us,
Are broken by Christ.
The walls are torn down
By the power of His life.
No prison can keep us
When we ask Him in.
He's ready to free us.
The question is when.

In Heaven's Light

She's in no prison.
Just ask her, she'll tell.
    Prosperity doctrine
    Has served her quite well.
She's paid her dues
And she's quick to say,
    That all's well in Zion,
    Now go on your way.

Her heart isn't stone.
Well, not before him.
    But now since he's hurt her,
    No others get in.
Refusing to trust,
She stands all alone.
    And she vows forgiveness,
    She'll never show.

His mom is demanding.
His father is gone.
    He can't find a love
    To which he belongs.
In the arms of a man
He seeks his release.
    But even with tolerance,
    He still can't find peace.

But the prisons that hold us,
Are broken by Christ.
The walls are torn down
By the power of His life.
No prison can keep us
When we ask Him in.
He's ready to free us.
The question is when.

In Heaven's Light

Did her mom ever love her?
She isn't quite sure.
    She couldn't remember
    Mom's love or nurture.
And father he tried,
But alas Dad was gone.
    So "No one cares!"
    Is the name of her song.

His eyes are blank hollows.
The brightness is gone.
    It doesn't take too much
    To see something's wrong.
He's kept plodding on,
Through years, oh, so sour.
    And no one could fault him
    If he threw in the towel.

She was a beauty,
At only sixteen.
    He took what he shouldn't,
    And then fled the scene.
Believing a lie,
She made a "choice."
    Now at the sight of a baby,
    Her eyes become moist.

But the prisons that hold us,
Are broken by Christ.
The walls are torn down
By the power of His life.
No prison can keep us
When we ask Him in.
He's ready to free us.
The question is when.

In Heaven's Light

He told her he loved her.
She wanted him to.
    And then they shared,
    What married folks do.
But what he gave her
Sure wasn't love.
    'Cause now no one will touch her
    Without a glove.

Her heart is so wounded
She won't even talk.
    The years of abuse
    Still haunt her and stalk.
Though he is now gone
And's been dead now for years
    His anger and hurtfulness
    Still can bring tears.

They want to be whole.
'Cause family's so dear.
    But theirs is still limping
    From pain and from fear.
Secrets have chained them
Within and without.
    And whether there's pure love,
    Still leaves them with doubt.

But the prisons that hold us,
Are broken by Christ.
The walls are torn down
By the power of His life.
No prison can keep us
When we ask Him in.
He's ready to free us.
The question is when.

In Heaven's Light

A pastor of many
But at home, it's a mess.
    He still does his job,
    But his life's quite the test.
His wife, though she loves him,
Is always at odds,
    Not just with his thinking
    But against his God.

The problem's not marriage.
The problem's not strife.
    It's not that we just can't
    Seem to get things right.
It's more like our focus
Is only on "us."
    While consumed with ourselves,
    We just missed the bus.

It's money. It's power.
It's looking our best.
    It's buying that new thing.
    It's passing that test.
"But I can see more!
So bless ME, dear Lord."
    And we wonder why
    Our soul's in discord.

But the prisons that hold us,
Are broken by Christ.
The walls are torn down
By the power of His life.
No prison can keep us
When we ask Him in.
He's ready to free us.
The question is when.

In Heaven's Light

ANY prison that holds you,

Is broken by Christ.

The walls are torn down

By the power of His life.

NO prison can keep you

When you ask Him in.

HE'S READY TO FREE <u>YOU</u>!

The question is, "When?"

©2006 Denise M. Barbour

Index by Topic

WE ARE INVITED

Come in Corporate Worship	59
Come into His Presence	23
Come to Me Early	51
God Given Name, A	58
Make a New Covenant	64
Meet Me in a Holy Place	15
Pray Like Angels	125
Shepherd, The	84
There's a Fire	130
There was a Cross	129
Your Walk, Our Walk, His Walk	112

WE ARE CALLED TO GROWTH AND TRANSFORMATION

Betrayed by the Body	41
Breathe on Me	95
Hard Living Transformation	74

In Heaven's Light

His Call	98
I Make All Things New	72
I Seek to be Transformed	111
If Something Were Left	21
Journey Toward New Life	60
New Life	62
Overcome Impurity	78
Prayer for Birth	75
Prayer Introspection	88
Pulse of Life, The	66
Purest Gold	50

WE ARE CALLED TO HIGHER UNDERSTANDING

Disillusioned Disciple	25
If We Knew…	52
Meat	83
My Face	56
Prayer Introspection	88
Stone to Throw	46
Wrestle	30

WE EXPERIENCE TRIALS

Betrayed by the Body	41
Don't Give Up	29
Gift in Trial	93
He's Most Near	81
I Trust in You, Lord	44
It Hurts	76
Life, a Never Ending Poem	102
Song of My Heart, The	27
Stand	127

Stone to Throw	46
Struggle	55
Too Many Trials	104
Touch the Thorn	106
Wrestle	30
You're the One I Need	54
You're Lying	86

WE WORSHIP THE ALMIGHTY

Come in Corporate Worship	59
Disillusioned Disciple	25
I Trust in You, Lord	44
Lord, I Love You	122
Morning Meeting	97
Morning Praise	37
Twenty-third Psalm Makeover–Shepherd to Parent	123
You're More than Dear	115
Your Image	43
Your Presence	80

WE LIVE IN FAMILY

Birth, New Life, Fresh Start	39
Graduate, The	91
Mother's Tribute to Her Children:, A	19
Thankfulness: A Choice	48
You're Lying	86

OTHER

Called by a New Name	70
Closer Than a Friend	118
Even to the Least	120

In Heaven's Light

First Sight of Baby	35
Hush	109
Prisons	132
Put on New Garments	68
Search Me	17
Second Witness of Christ?	100
Treasure Offering	90
Twenty-third Psalm Makeover–Shepherd to Parent	123
Words from the Vine	13

ALPHABETICAL INDEX

Betrayed by the Body	41
Birth, New Life, Fresh Start	39
Breathe on Me	95
Called by a New Name	70
Closer Than a Friend	118
Come in Corporate Worship	59
Come into His Presence	23
Come to Me Early	51
Disillusioned Disciple	25
Don't Give Up	29
Even to the Least	120
First Sight of Baby	35
Gift in Trial	93
God Given Name, A	58
Graduate, The	91

Hard Living Transformation	74
He's Most Near	81
His Call	98
Hush	109
I Make All Things New	72
I Seek to be Transformed	111
I Trust in You, Lord	44
If We Knew…	52
If Something Were Left	21
It Hurts	76
Journey Toward New Life	60
Life, a Never Ending Poem	102
Lord, I Love You	122
Make a New Covenant	64
Meat	83
Meet Me in a Holy Place	15
Morning Meeting	97
Morning Praise	37
Mother's Tribute to Her Children:, A	19
My Face	56
New Life	62
Overcome Impurity	78
Pray Like Angels	125
Prayer for Birth	75
Prayer Introspection	88

In Heaven's Light

Prisons	132
Pulse of Life, The	66
Purest Gold	50
Put on New Garments	68
Search Me	17
Second Witness of Christ?, A	100
Shepherd, The	84
Song of My Heart, The	27
Stand	127
Stone to Throw, A	46
Struggle	55
Thankfulness: A Choice	48
There was a Cross	129
There's a Fire	130
Too Many Trials	104
Touch the Thorn	106
Treasure Offering	90
Twenty-third Psalm Makeover–Shepherd to Parent	123
Words from the Vine	13
Wrestle	30
You're Lying	86
You're More Than Dear	115
You're the One I Need	54
Your Image	43
Your Presence	80
Your Walk, Our Walk, His Walk	112

In Heaven's Light

Order Form

Use this form to order additional copies

Please print:

Name _____

Address _____

City _____ State _____

Zip _____

Phone _____

Email _____

_____ copies of book @ $15.99 each $_____

Postage and handling @ $ 4.50 per book $_____

                    Total amount enclosed $_____

Make checks payable to Denise Barbour

Send to:
Denise Barbour, PO Box 10843, Jackson, TN 38308

Pleasant Word

To order additional copies of this title call:
1-877-421-READ (7323)
or please visit our Web site at
www.pleasantwordbooks.com

If you enjoyed this quality custom-published book,
drop by our Web site for more books and information.

www.winepressgroup.com
"Your partner in custom publishing."

Printed in the United States
123241LV00010B/1-18/P